OUR LIVING WORLD

Fish

By **Edward R. Ricciuti**

With Illustrations by William Simpson

Series Editor: Vincent Marteka

Introduction by John Behler, *New York Zoological Society*

A BLACKBIRCH PRESS BOOK

WOODBRIDGE, CONNECTICUT

Published by Blackbirch Press, Inc.
One Bradley Road, Suite 205
Woodbridge, CT 06525

©1993 Blackbirch Press, Inc.
First Edition

Printed in Canada

10 9 8 7 6 5 4 3 2 1

Editorial Director: Bruce Glassman
Editor: Geraldine C. Fox
Editorial Assistant: Michelle Spinelli
Design Director: Sonja Kalter
Production: Sandra Burr, Rudy Raccio

Library of Congress Cataloging-in-Publication Data

Ricciuti, Edward R.
    Fish / by Edward R. Ricciuti.—1st ed.
        p.   cm. — (Our living world)
    Includes bibliographical references and index.
    Summary: Examines the physical structure, metabolism, and life cycle of fishes and discusses how they fit into the food chain.
    ISBN 1-56711-041-X   ISBN 1-56711-056-8 (Trade)
    1. Fishes—Juvenile literature. [1. Fishes.] I. Title. II. Series.
QL617.2.R52   1993
597—dc20   92-44038
                                                                     CIP
                                                                      AC

Contents

What Does It Mean to Be "Alive"?

Introduction by John Behler,
New York Zoological Society

One summer morning, as I was walking through a beautiful field, I was inspired to think about what it really means to be "alive." Part of the answer, I came to realize, was right in front of my eyes.

The meadow was ablaze with color, packed with wildflowers at the height of their blooming season. A multitude of insects, warmed by the sun's early-morning rays, began to stir. Painted turtles sunned themselves on an old mossy log in a nearby pond. A pair of wood ducks whistled a call as they flew overhead, resting near a shagbark hickory on the other side of the pond.

As I wandered through this unspoiled habitat, I paused at a patch of milkweed to look for monarch-butterfly caterpillars, which depend on the milkweed's leaves for food. Indeed, the caterpillars were there, munching away. Soon these larvae would spin their cocoons, emerge as beautiful orange-and-black butterflies, and begin a fantastic 1,500-mile (2,400-kilometer) migration to wintering grounds in Mexico. It took biologists nearly one hundred years to unravel the life history of these butterflies. Watching them in the milkweed patch made me wonder how much more there is to know about these insects and all the other living organisms in just that one meadow.

The patterns of the natural world have often been likened to a spider's web, and for good reason. All life on Earth is interconnected in an elegant yet surprisingly simple design, and each living thing is an essential part of that design. To understand biology and the functions of living things, biologists have spent a lot of time looking at the differences among organisms. But in order to understand the very nature of living things, we must first understand what they have in common.

The butterfly larvae and the milkweed—and all animals and plants, for that matter—are made up of the same basic elements. These elements are obtained, used, and eliminated by every living thing in a series of chemical activities called metabolism.

Every molecule of every living tissue must contain carbon. During photosynthesis, green plants take in carbon dioxide from the atmosphere. Within their chlorophyll-filled leaves, in the presence of sunlight, the carbon dioxide is combined with water to form sugar—nature's most basic food. Animals need carbon, too. To grow and function, animals must eat plants or other animals that have fed on plants in order to obtain carbon. When plants and animals die, bacteria and fungi help to break down their tissues. This allows the carbon in plants and animals to be recycled. Indeed, the carbon in your body—and everyone else's body—may once have been inside a dinosaur, a giant redwood, or a monarch butterfly!

All life also needs nitrogen. Nitrogen is an essential component of protoplasm, the complex of chemicals that makes up living cells. Animals acquire nitrogen in the same manner as they acquire carbon dioxide: by eating plants or other animals that have eaten plants. Plants, however, must rely on nitrogen-fixing bacteria in the soil to absorb nitrogen from the atmosphere and convert it into proteins. These proteins are then absorbed from the soil by plant roots.

Living things start life as a single cell. The process by which cells grow and reproduce to become a specific organism—whether the organism is an oak tree or a whale—is controlled by two basic substances called deoxyribonucleic acid (DNA) and ribonucleic acid (RNA). These two chemicals are the building blocks of genes that determine how an organism looks, grows, and functions. Each organism has a unique pattern of DNA and RNA in its genes. This pattern determines all the characteristics of a living thing. Each species passes its unique pattern from generation to generation. Over many billions of years, a process involving genetic mutation and natural selection has allowed species to adapt to a constantly changing environment by evolving—changing genetic patterns. The living creatures we know today are the results of these adaptations.

Reproduction and growth are important to every species, since these are the processes by which new members of a species are created. If a species cannot reproduce and adapt, or if it cannot reproduce fast enough to replace those members that die, it will become extinct (no longer exist).

In recent years, biologists have learned a great deal about how living things function. But there is still much to learn about nature. With high-technology equipment and new information, exciting discoveries are being made every day. New insights and theories quickly make many biology textbooks obsolete. One thing, however, will forever remain certain: As living things, we share an amazing number of characteristics with other forms of life. As animals, our survival depends upon the food and functions provided by other animals and plants. As humans—who can understand the similarities and interdependence among living things—we cannot help but feel connected to the natural world, and we cannot forget our responsibility to protect it. It is only through looking at, and understanding, the rest of the natural world that we can truly appreciate what it means to be "alive."

1

Fishes: The Overview

Are fishes special? You bet they are. Their story goes back almost a half billion years. Then, in the ancient ocean, life on Earth took a giant step forward. A new kind of animal developed there. It was the first animal that had an internal skeleton. This skeleton was built around a backbone. The new animal was a fish.

The Bony Skeleton

A skeleton is the framework that supports a body. Bones give a body shape. The skeleton of an animal grows along with the body. As far as skeletons are concerned, fish and humans are actually quite similar. Both fish and humans have an internal skeleton with a backbone.

The most important part of your skeleton is the backbone. It is often called the "spine." Inside it are nerves linking your brain with the rest of your body. They carry messages back and forth between your

brain and your body parts. Your backbone protects these nerves.

The growth of a skeleton and backbone allowed certain animals to develop complex nervous systems. That is why the first animal with a backbone is so important in the history of life.

The backbone itself is made of smaller bones called vertebrae. That is why backboned animals are called "vertebrates." There are four other groups of vertebrates besides fishes: amphibians, reptiles, birds, and mammals (humans are part of the mammal category). All these other vertebrates can trace their ancestry to the first vertebrates: fishes.

The size and shape of fishes depend on the environment in which they live. The three most common shapes for fishes are flat, round, and tubular. The peacock flounder *(far left)*, which lives on—and feeds from—the ocean floor, is flat in order to blend into its surroundings. The butterfly fish *(left)* has a shape that is best adapted for swimming through tight spaces. The tubular lamprey *(above)* is best adapted for weaving in and out of rocky crevices, looking for food.

The Dazzling Variety of Fishes

Being the first vertebrates is not the only honor that fishes can claim. They also make up the largest group of vertebrates. Almost half of all the living species of vertebrates are fishes. Fishes number more than 25,000 species. And scientists have been discovering about 100 more species each year. By way of comparison, there are only about 4,000 species of mammals.

The differences among fishes are truly dazzling. When it comes to size, shape, and behavior, fishes are quite varied. The smallest fish is the pygmy goby. It is no longer than a pencil eraser. The biggest fish is

Fishes: The Overview

the whale shark. How big? Think of two basketball courts, placed end to end. The whale shark is longer.

Many fish are torpedo-shaped. But others are flat as pancakes, round as balloons, or long like ribbons. A few even look like boxes.

The life-styles of fishes are as varied as their shapes and sizes. As its name suggests, the mouth-breeder shelters its young inside its mouth. The bright little jawfish uses its mouth as a shovel to dig a burrow in the sandy bottom. It lines the burrow with pebbles to prevent collapse. The jawfish piles extra pebbles near the entrance to its burrow. The pile must be guarded like a treasure. If not, other jawfish will sneak up, raid it, and escape with a mouthful of pebbles.

The Water World

Fishes inhabit almost all of the Earth's waters. And there is plenty of water for them. Almost three quarters of the Earth's surface lies under water. Most of it is ocean. Many parts of the ocean are deeper than any land is high. If the tallest mountain in the world could be put into the deepest part of the ocean, its peak would be more than a mile underwater!

The vast world of water has countless different habitats (living places), each with its unique environment. Different fishes have adapted to these varied habitats. Some fishes dwell in the lightless ocean depths. Others cruise near the sea's sunlit surface. Some even inhabit hot springs that can reach 100 degrees F. (38 degrees C.). Still others swim through the subfreezing temperatures of the Antarctic Ocean. And still others live in puddles that seasonally go dry. You can find fishes in rushing rivers, desert pools, and lakes that can be up to 15,000 feet (4,575 meters) high in the mountains.

Opposite:
The vast world of the ocean contains almost an infinite number of habitats. Different species of fishes have adapted to life at particular ocean depths. The most commonly known fishes live toward the surface of the ocean. These fishes include marlin, tuna, mackerel, and sardines. Fishes such as certain sharks, rays, and barracudas live farther beneath the ocean's surface. Even lower are such fishes as the oarfish, the umbrella-mouth gulper eel, and the tripod fish.

SARDINES

SHARK

MACKERELS

Ocean Habitats

RAY

OARFISH

HATCHET FISH

LANTERN FISH

BRISTLEMOUTH

UMBRELLA-MOUTH GULPER EEL

TRIPOD FISH

COMMON BLACKDEVIL
DEEP-SEA ANGLER

What All Fishes Share

Because of the many differences among fishes, it is difficult to describe a typical fish. There is really only one thing for sure about fishes. Almost anything you can say about them has exceptions.

Scales, for instance, are a fish trademark. They are usually clear and feel like plastic. Overlapping scales cover the skin of many fishes. They toughen and protect the skin, like a flexible suit of armor. But some fishes lack scales. The swordfish and huge ocean sunfish do not have them. Neither does the lamprey.

Although not all fishes have scales, fishes do share a few basic features, like fins. Fins help a fish swim and steer. Kinds of fins and how they are used differ among species. Generally, a fish has several types of fins. The fin along a fish's back is called the dorsal fin. Its counterpart underneath the fish is the anal fin. These fins act like the keel of a boat. They help to stabilize the fish. Other fins are paired. Fins behind the head, one on each side, are the pectoral fins. Those in front of the anal fin are the pelvic fins. The pectoral and pelvic fins are used for maneuvering in the water.

Organs called gills are another common feature of fishes. Gills enable fishes to breathe underwater. Gills are usually just rear of the eye, on each side of a fish's body.

The Three Groups of Fishes

Scientists divide fishes into three major groups. The smallest group includes only a handful of species. Snake-like in form, they are very primitive. That's why scientists call this group the primitive fishes. Many scientists think these fishes, the jawless fishes, were among the very first fishes. The jawless fishes got their name because they lack jawbones and can't bite. Instead, they have round mouths that work like suckers.

The lamprey is a common jawless fish. Within its mouth is a tongue covered with teeth, like a file. To feed, the lamprey fastens its mouth to a bigger fish. Then, using its tongue, it scrapes through the prey's skin. The lamprey then drinks its victim's blood.

The skeleton of sharks, rays, and their kin, as well as jawless fishes, is not true bone. Instead, it is made of a bone-like material called cartilage. Although it is similar to bone, cartilage is not as hard and is more elastic. To feel an example of cartilage, touch the tip of your nose. That flexible material under the skin is cartilage.

Sharks, rays, and their relatives make up the second scientific group of fishes. This group is called the cartilaginous fishes. Cartilaginous fishes include about 600 species. Their ancestors were the first fishes with biting jaws. An unusual member of this group is the sawfish. It can grow to 20 feet (6 meters) in length. Its snout is long and is edged with sharp teeth. The sawfish uses this weapon to kill prey by slashing at groups of smaller fishes.

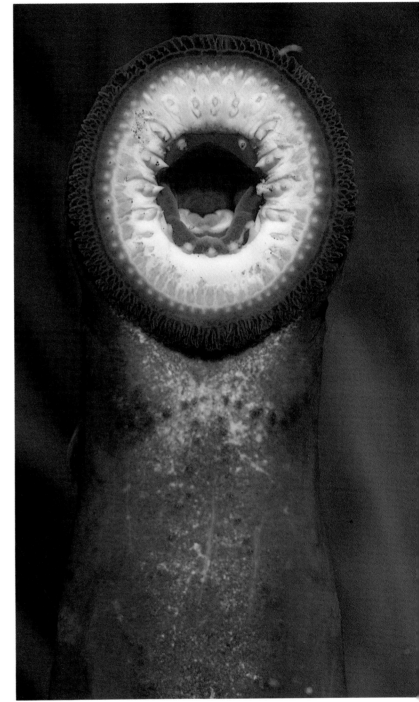

A lamprey raises its head and opens its mouth. The lamprey is a common, primitive jawless fish. To feed, the lamprey uses its tongue to scrape through the skin of its victims so it can drink their blood.

Different Kinds of Fishes

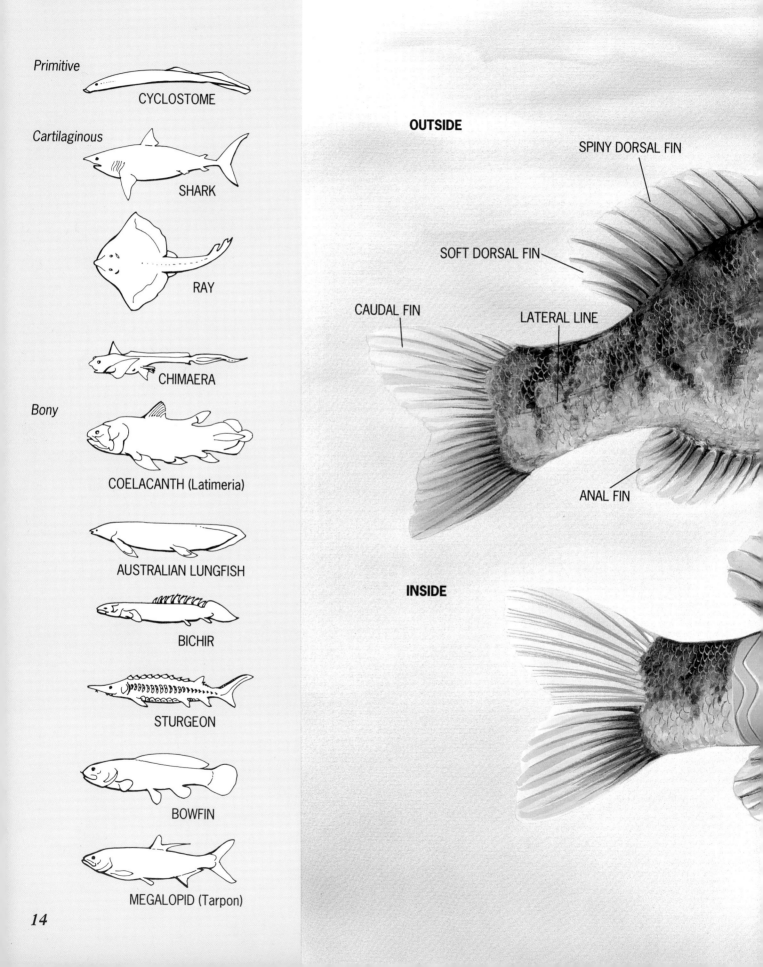

Primitive

CYCLOSTOME

Cartilaginous

SHARK

RAY

CHIMAERA

Bony

COELACANTH (Latimeria)

AUSTRALIAN LUNGFISH

BICHIR

STURGEON

BOWFIN

MEGALOPID (Tarpon)

OUTSIDE

SPINY DORSAL FIN

SOFT DORSAL FIN

CAUDAL FIN

LATERAL LINE

ANAL FIN

INSIDE

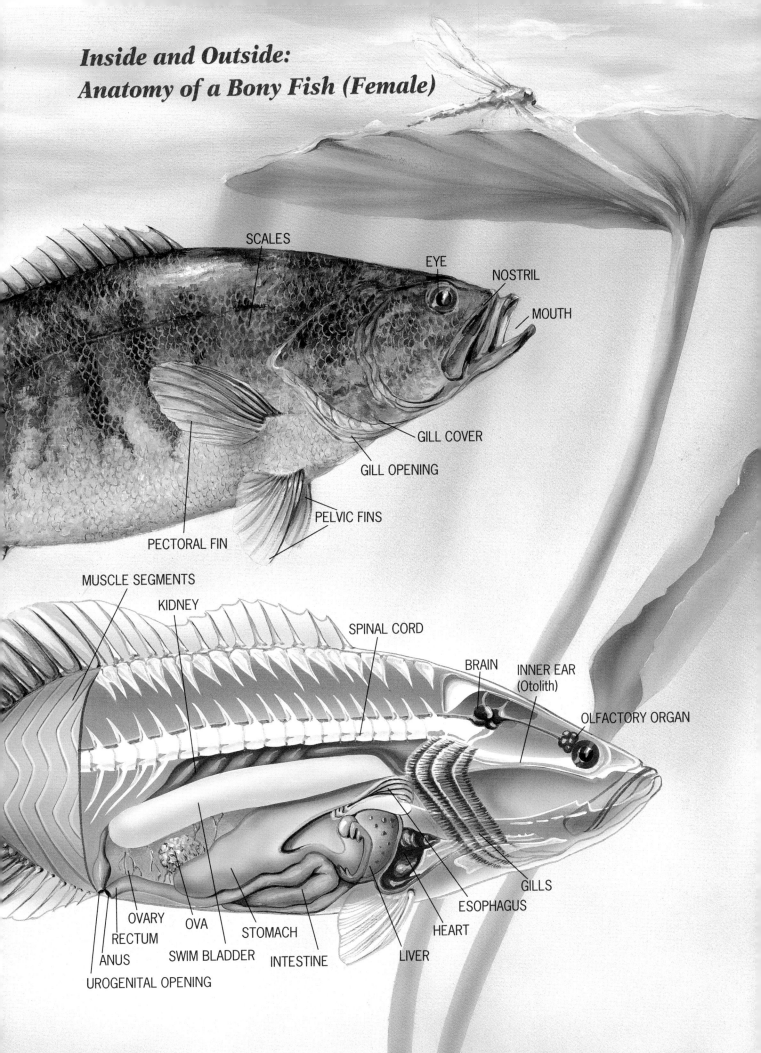

Inside and Outside:
Anatomy of a Bony Fish (Female)

SCALES

EYE

NOSTRIL

MOUTH

GILL COVER

GILL OPENING

PELVIC FINS

PECTORAL FIN

MUSCLE SEGMENTS

KIDNEY

SPINAL CORD

BRAIN

INNER EAR
(Otolith)

OLFACTORY ORGAN

GILLS

ESOPHAGUS

HEART

LIVER

INTESTINE

STOMACH

SWIM BLADDER

OVA

OVARY

RECTUM

ANUS

UROGENITAL OPENING

Sharks are the most common members of the group of fishes known as the cartilaginous fishes.

The bony fishes are the largest group of fishes. They are the most advanced and have a skeleton of real bone, like humans. Goldfishes, guppies, tunas, trout, bluegills, and bass are all bony fishes. So are catfishes, sailfishes, eels, and cod.

The Swim Bladder

Most of the bony fishes—but not all—have an internal organ called a swim bladder. This is a float that helps the fish rise, sink, or stay in place.

The swim bladder is basically a gas bag. It works like a hot-air balloon. When it expands with gas, the fish rises in the water. When it shrinks, the fish sinks. Some fishes—trout, for instance—inflate their swim bladder by gulping air at the surface. Most fill the bladder with oxygen from the water. By controlling the amount of gas in the bladder, a fish can hang at a particular depth with hardly any effort. It is as if the fish becomes weightless.

How Fishes Swim

Most fishes swim with sideways movements of the tail fin. The tail gets its power from muscles along the length of the fish's body. Starting at the head, these muscles tighten and relax very quickly, too fast for the human eye to see. Fishes with rigid bodies, such as trunkfishes, rely mostly on their pectoral fins for swimming.

A swim bladder is a big advantage to a fish. Fishes without swim bladders, such as sharks, must move continuously, or they will sink. Moving constantly takes lots of energy. Perhaps that is why sharks are such hearty eaters. The more energy an animal needs, the more food it needs to fuel its body processes.

Fish Shapes

You can tell much about the way a fish lives by its shape. Streamlined fishes that are shaped like torpedoes swim the fastest. Swordfish can swim at 60 miles (97 kilometers) an hour. Tunas go a bit more slowly. The mako shark is just as speedy. A streamlined form is ideal for moving through water. Water resists movement more than air because water is 800 times more dense than air. When a fish swims, it has to push water aside like a wedge. A streamlined form

The largest group of fishes is the bony fishes. They have skeletons made up of real bone. The bony fishes are the ones that are most commonly known, such as goldfishes, guppies, trout, bass, and catfishes (shown here).

The streamlined shape of the barracuda makes it a very fast swimmer. Its body is designed for quick bursts of speed, which can reach up to 25 miles (40 kilometers) an hour.

Gravity Fighter
Water's high density provides support for animals that live in water. It holds them up. Land animals rely on their muscles and skeleton to keep them from collapsing. The larger an animal gets, the more difficult it is to grow and support an internal framework. That is why the largest animals that ever lived, the great whales, evolved in water. Not even the dinosaurs were as large as the blue whale, which can grow up to 100 feet (31 meters) long and weigh over 300,000 pounds (136,000 kilograms)!

slips through water more easily than does a bulky form. Torpedo-shaped fishes mainly live in open water, often far out at sea. They are usually predators that chase down their prey. Many are long-distance travelers. Some cover many thousands of miles a year.

The barracuda is streamlined, too. But it is shaped more like an arrow than a torpedo. Built for a quick burst of speed, it can travel up to 25 miles (40 kilometers) an hour. The barracuda uses its swim bladder and fins to hang suspended in the water, motionless. The fish is so streamlined that, head on, it is almost invisible. The barracuda also has keen eyes. When it sees a smaller fish, it erupts into motion. Its broad tail gives it an explosive shove forward. The barracuda then rockets toward its prey and grabs it with long, pointed teeth.

Flatfishes generally spend much of their time on or near the bottom of their habitat. The flounder is an example. It lies quietly, hiding from predators that want to eat it and from animals it wants to eat. The flounder does not chase food. It waits for a meal to come near. Then it jumps after the prey. The flounder's flat body gives it a quick lift off the bottom. That is all it needs to catch its food.

Stand a pancake on end, and you have another type of fish shape. It is flat on each side. Head on, it looks like the rim of a dinner plate—very thin. The butterfly fish has this type of body. It lives on coral reefs. The freshwater angelfish, popular for home aquariums, is another example.

Neither the butterfly fish nor the angelfish lives in open water. Butterfly fishes inhabit coral reefs that are honeycombed with cracks and crannies. Sponges, sea fans, and sea whips grow on coral. These are animals that actually look like plants. In fact, they form what looks like an underwater forest rooted in the coral.

The angelfish lives in shallow parts of South American rivers. Aquatic plants thrive in the shallows. They grow upward toward the sun in thick masses.

The habitats of the angelfish and the butterfly fish are very similar. Each is an underwater jungle. The aquatic plants and plant-like animals in their habitats grow vertically. The thin bodies of the butterfly fish and angelfish can slide between the plants. Strong

The thin, flat body of the butterfly fish enables it to slide between the aquatic plants and coral reefs that are common in its habitat.

A Fish out of Water

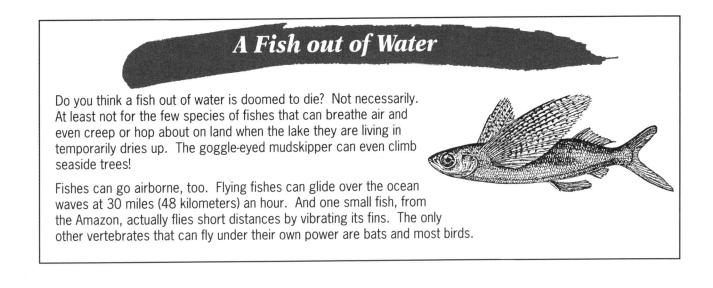

Do you think a fish out of water is doomed to die? Not necessarily. At least not for the few species of fishes that can breathe air and even creep or hop about on land when the lake they are living in temporarily dries up. The goggle-eyed mudskipper can even climb seaside trees!

Fishes can go airborne, too. Flying fishes can glide over the ocean waves at 30 miles (48 kilometers) an hour. And one small fish, from the Amazon, actually flies short distances by vibrating its fins. The only other vertebrates that can fly under their own power are bats and most birds.

fins, always moving, help them turn on a dime. Their head-on profile is so thin that an enemy can hardly see them. The angelfish even has natural camouflage. Vertical stripes on its sides look like the plants among which it hides.

Coral reefs are also the home of the moray eel, an aggressive predator. A moray eel can reach up to 6 feet (2 meters) long. It has powerful jaws and long, sharp teeth. Its snake-like body is very flexible. This shape is ideal for the way the moray lives.

The moray can wind through holes in the reef. There, it can hide from enemies while it also finds its food, mostly small octopuses and crabs. Every animal in nature is equipped with certain advantages and certain disadvantages. Each animal balances those qualities in order to survive. A moray eel, for example, could never surpass a mako shark in speed or distance. But a mako could never get into the holes through which a moray travels with ease.

A pufferfish looks like a miniature blimp. When it is threatened, it inflates itself. Sharp spines cover

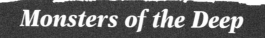

Monsters of the Deep

Fishes that live in the ocean depths, where no light penetrates, can look like "monsters from another planet." Many have gaping jaws and long, curved teeth. Some make their own light, much as a firefly does.

These fish may look like large monsters, but they really are small animals. Most are only 1 to 2 feet (30 to 61 centimeters) long. But their world is much like another planet. At the bottom of the ocean, it is icy cold and forever dark. Miles below the water's surface, many of these animals survive on matter that falls to the ocean floor. The water pressure, that deep in the ocean, is so great that it would crush a human body almost instantly.

The moray eel lives in a habitat filled with coral reefs. Its flexible snake-like body enables it to wind through the tight spaces inside the coral in search of food. Its powerful jaws and long, sharp teeth also make it a very effective predator.

its body. Puffed up, it is a prickly mouthful for enemies. The trunkfish has a boxy body. An armor of thick plates protects it. Its body is rigid, not flexible like that of most other fishes.

The pufferfish uses its body shape to defend itself against enemies. It inflates itself when threatened. Because its body is covered with prickly spines, the inflated pufferfish becomes hard for a predator to eat.

Shape is only one of the many factors that have enabled fishes to adapt to the water world. Some of these adaptations may seem weird to you, but in the vast and varied world of the ocean, they are as normal as fingers and toes are to us.

2

The Senses: How Fishes React

Fishes have the same five senses that humans have. They are the same basic senses that all other vertebrates have. Like humans, fish use their eyes for seeing, ears for hearing, nostrils for smelling, taste buds for tasting, and nerve endings for detecting touch or feeling.

A fish also has two additional senses especially suited to water. The high density of water makes it an excellent carrier of vibrations. A fish can detect vibrations from moving objects. This sense is like a "distant touch," but it can also be described as "feeling" sound.

Water is also a super transmitter of electricity. The body of a vertebrate generates tiny electrical charges when it signals muscles to contract. Some fishes have finely tuned senses that feel these charges.

Opposite:
A cutthroat trout searches the water for food. Like humans, fishes use the five basic senses of sight, hearing, touch, taste, and smell to take in information about their surroundings.

The Nervous System of a Fish

A fish's nervous system, like that of other vertebrates, consists of a brain, a spinal cord, and nerves. Some nerves, called sensory nerves, carry messages from the sense organs to the brain through the spinal cord. Other nerves, called motor nerves, then carry messages from the brain through the spinal cord to the muscles.

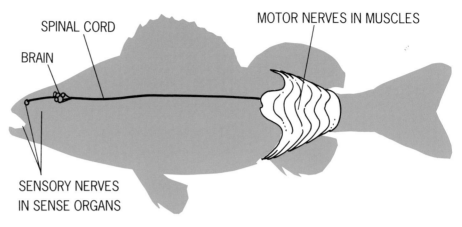

SPINAL CORD

BRAIN

MOTOR NERVES IN MUSCLES

SENSORY NERVES IN SENSE ORGANS

Senses and Behavior

An animal's senses constantly gather information about its surroundings. Senses react to a never-ending flood of messages, called stimuli.

These messages are relayed to an animal's brain. Once a message reaches the brain, an animal reacts with various kinds of behavior. The type of reaction depends on the message.

Think about what happens if you touch something very hot. In an instant, your hand yanks back from the heat. Nerve endings in your fingers feel pain. This unpleasant message flashes in microseconds through your nervous system to your brain. It replies instantly with a message that tells your hand to "move away fast." So it moves. All these activities occur like lightning. They're so fast that you don't really feel as though you're thinking about it. You just do it.

Animals also have certain reactions that are not automatic; they are learned. When you are feeling for a light switch in the dark, for example, your brain is thinking. Once you touch the switch, your brain, based on experience, reasons that you have found the switch. The next thing you do is flip the switch on.

A fish probably cannot "reason" the way a human does. Most of a fish's reactions to the information it receives from the senses are reflexes. These are automatic patterns of behavior that are inherited from an animal's ancestors.

The sudden appearance of a large shape, for instance, may switch on "escape behavior" in small fishes. When they see the shape, they automatically scoot away from it. They don't really think about danger. They just react to the shape.

Fishing lures take advantage of a fish's reflex behavior. Some arouse feeding behavior and others provoke aggressive behavior. Sometimes, however, even the designers of a lure do not know what to expect. They just know that fishes will strike it.

Habitat and the Senses

The sense on which a fish relies most heavily often depends on its habitat. Most fishes depend on vision to keep them aware of their immediate surroundings. The sharpest eyes belong to fishes that live in clear water, especially species that are active predators. Many fishes that have adapted to living in murky water find food by smell, taste, and touch. Several species of small fishes that live in dark caves or at the very bottom of the ocean are blind. But their hearing is very sensitive. Some fishes, such as the largemouth bass, use several senses equally well. Because of this, bass can live under a wide variety of conditions in many different habitats.

How Fishes See

Fish eyes and human eyes have a similar structure. Both kinds of eyes work the same way, like a camera. Light enters through a clear center in the eye, called the lens. The light then registers an image on the

DID YOU KNOW

Learning out of Hand

Although reasoning seems beyond them, fishes can learn. Some goldfishes, for example, can learn to associate a hand or an arm above their aquarium with the act of feeding. They can learn this if they are fed each time they see a hand. Eventually, feeding behavior becomes a reflex to the sight of a hand. Scientists call these predictable reactions "learned behavior."

The Eye of a Fish

Although fishes are basically nearsighted, they can focus somewhat over short distances. A muscle attached to the lens pulls the lens in, flattening it and allowing a fish to focus on more distant objects.

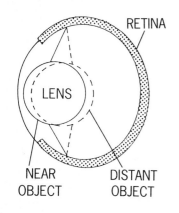

RETINA

LENS

NEAR
OBJECT

DISTANT
OBJECT

retina, a coating at the back of the eye. The retina can be compared to film in a camera. The optic nerve transmits the image to the brain, where it is then "developed."

Covering the lens is the iris. It channels light into the eye. A human iris also regulates the amount of light entering the lens. It has an expandable hole in the center. The hole widens as light levels decrease and shrinks as light increases.

The hole in a fish's iris always remains the same size. It cannot adjust to different light levels. That is the job of cells in the fish's retina.

During the night, the surface of the retina contains large numbers of cells called rods. They are powerful light receptors that can detect very dim light. In bright light, rods are overpowered. By day, rods sink inside the retina and are replaced by other cells called cones. Cones are not as sensitive to light as rods. But they don't need to be, because they work in bright light.

The switch of rods to cones is a gradual process. Rods start to surface from within the retina as darkness sets in. They begin sinking back as daylight approaches and cones slowly replace them.

How Far Can a Fish See?

Fishes are nearsighted (they see nearby objects best) because their eye lens is not flexible. A human lens bulges to focus on close objects and flattens for distance. But a fish's lens is locked in a bulge.

A fish's eye, however, can focus somewhat over short distances. To do so, it uses a muscle attached to its lens. The closer the muscle pulls the lens toward the retina, the flatter it gets, and the farther the fish can see. Even so, most fishes cannot see beyond about 50 feet (15 meters).

An Eye for an Eye

A fish's eyes are located on the sides of its head. Eyes in this position can see left, right, straight ahead, and up and down. Together, a fish's two eyes can see almost a complete circle. And the fish doesn't even have to move!

The exact placement of a fish's eyes determines its field of vision. The eyes of a bass have a forward position. This setup is better for seeing what's ahead and best suits a fish that chases other fishes. The bass also has excellent depth perception, which helps to keep it on target when striking prey.

A minnow's eyes are farther back than a bass's. If you were a minnow, your eyes would be where your ears are. This means a minnow's field of vision does not extend as far forward as a bass's. The minnow, therefore, is not as good at telling distances. But a minnow can see almost all around itself, including what's behind it. This comes in very handy when the minnow has a hungry bass on its tail!

Nearsightedness is not a problem for fishes. Light does not penetrate water as easily as air. And water is filled with suspended particles that obscure light. Even in the clearest water, seeing for 100 feet (31 meters) is considered exceptional. In murky water, visibility is very poor. That is why fishes have little need for long-distance vision. They use vision up close only and depend on other senses at long range.

Fishes and Sound

Humans can hear a much greater range of sound than fishes. Although both fishes and humans can hear a similar amount of low-frequency sounds, humans can hear sounds of much higher pitch than fishes.

Within its range, however, a fish can hear very well. And, because water is so dense, it conducts sound five times faster than air. This makes it easier for a fish to hear sounds at great distances.

How Fishes Hear

You can't see a fish's ears. They are completely within its head. The fish's ear is basically a sac that contains fluids and is lined with tiny hairs. It is very similar to

DID YOU KNOW

Fishes Don't Cry

A fish's eye lacks tear ducts. Since they live in water, fishes do not need tears to moisten their eyes. Nor do they need eyelids to retain moisture.

the inner ear of a human, but it is much simpler. That is because the more complex ear of higher vertebrates evolved from that of a fish.

Fishes, unlike humans, do not have eardrums. Vibrations flow from water through a fish's head into its ear sac. These vibrations move through the fluids in its ears. The hairs in the sac pick up the vibrations. The auditory (hearing) nerve transmits the vibrations to the fish's brain.

Humans have three small bones in their ears that amplify sound. But the ear of a fish lacks these three bones. A large number of fishes, however, use their swim bladder as an amplifier. Such fishes include minnows, catfishes, and herrings. Their swim bladders pick up sound vibrations. As the bladder then resonates, like a drum head, the sound grows louder and is transmitted to the ear.

The Lateral Line

Sounds that fishes cannot hear with their ears can still be sensed by many fishes. A special sense organ called the lateral line receives subsonic (very low) vibrations from moving objects. The lateral line

Fishes use their lateral line to pick up subsonic (very low) sounds that they cannot hear with their ears. The lateral line runs down the middle of the body, from the head all the way down to the tail.

The Senses: How Fishes React

Mistaken Identity

A barracuda feeds mostly on small fishes. It grabs its prey and eats it as it swims. Once in a while, however, barracudas attack people. Usually these attacks involve only one bite before the barracuda vanishes.

A person is too large for the barracuda's hit-and-run method of feeding. And a human swimmer looks nothing like a small fish. So why should a barracuda attack a person?

It is probably a case of mistaken identity. A shiny bracelet on a swimmer's wrist or a moving foot may send the same stimulus to the barracuda's eye as would a small fish. The shiny object may trigger a reflex feeding response in the barracuda. So the barracuda zips in, grabs the "fish," and takes off. It does not know it has bitten a human instead of a fish, even though humans look nothing like fishes!

operates much like the ear, picking up vibrations and sending messages to the brain. It is a network of small canals that are under the skin and along each side of the fish. Filled with mucus, the canals contain small hairs that resemble those inside the ear. The canals open to the water through tiny pores.

Vibrations pass from the water through the pores into the mucus. As in the ear, the mucus moves, and the hairs pick up the vibrations. Nerves attached to the hairs then relay the information to the brain.

The lateral line is a medium-range sense organ. In many fishes, it can detect vibrations from about 30 feet (9 meters) away. Some can sense vibrations from three times that distance. The lateral line helps detect food and predators. It also aids navigation. Vibrations from a fish that bounce off underwater objects can be received by its own lateral line. Only fishes and a few amphibians (animals that develop from water-breathers to air-breathers) have a lateral line.

The Sense of Smell

Smell is the ability to detect odors produced by chemicals. Both water and air carry odors, but water holds odors better than air. Currents in water can

DID YOU KNOW

Fishy Sounds Sound Fishy

Sound is a vibration that the ear can hear. Vibrations cannot travel through a vacuum. Only something that has density, such as air or water, can carry sound. The density of water is excellent for transmitting sound. If you are underwater when two stones are struck, you can easily hear the sound. Sound travels 1 mile (2 kilometers) a minute through water.

Fishes can make many sounds. Some fishes produce sounds by vibrating their swim bladders. Others grind their teeth. Some even rattle their bones. The water can be an awfully noisy place!

carry odors over great distances. Avoiding predators or finding prey is easier for a fish with a good sense of smell. Many fish use their ability to smell as a long-distance sense, like hearing.

Just as in most of the air-breathing vertebrates, the cells that detect odors (olfactory cells) are in a fish's nostrils. Humans have nostrils, too. They are in the nose. A fish doesn't have a nose, but it does have nostrils on each side of its snout.

Fishes don't have noses, but they do have nostrils on both sides of their snouts. They rely on their sense of smell for many functions, including finding food.

Some fishes have an incredible sense of smell. American and European eels can smell even a single molecule of certain chemicals in millions of gallons of water. They are also among the fishes that can best sense odors over immense distances. Smell leads them to their breeding grounds by guiding them to places that may be as far away as 4,000 miles (6,400 kilometers)!

Sharks can sense the odor of a trace of blood in millions of gallons of water. That's not surprising. Two thirds of the cells in a shark's brain are in some way responsible for the shark's sense of smell.

Scientists have plugged the nostrils of certain catfishes and put them into a tank of clear water. The fish were unable to find food in the tank even though they saw it. Those results showed how much fishes rely upon their sense of smell.

A Fish of Many Colors

Rods register only black and white. Cones are sensitive to color. Most fishes can see colors, but color vision depends on the species. What happens to a fish's color vision at night when the cones recede? It is gone. But that doesn't matter. As the amount of sunlight decreases, colors vanish from the water.

"White" sunlight is a mix of colors. When it grows dark, reds disappear from the water first, then oranges. Greens and blues linger, but they, too, finally fade.

The same thing happens as sunlight penetrates water. Water absorbs colors as it gets deeper. The color red disappears past 30 feet (9 meters) below the water's surface. Greens and blues are the last to disappear. They are not lost until about 300 hundred feet (92 meters) below the surface of the water.

Fishes living in shallow water generally have the greatest range of color vision. That makes sense, because most colors are still visible in shallow depths. Deepwater fishes can detect fewer colors, mostly greens and blues. That makes sense, too. Blues and greens are the dominant colors where those fishes live.

Most fishes have taste buds in their mouths as well as on the outsides of their mouths or on their snouts. Carp are among the fishes that have taste buds scattered all along their bodies.

The Sense of Taste

Smell and taste are closely related. Taste buds are cells that also sense chemicals. Human taste buds are on the tongue and roof of the mouth. So are a fish's. But most species also have taste buds outside their mouths.

External taste buds in fishes are usually on the lips, snout, or feelers (called barbels), which extend from the snout. Carp are among the fishes that have taste buds scattered all around their bodies.

Taste, like vision, is a close-up sense in fishes. Smell may lead a catfish to food, but a potential meal is generally confirmed by taste. A catfish constantly probes around the bottom with its barbels, tasting for possible food.

The Sense of Touch

The feelers of a catfish also contain nerve endings sensitive to touch. How much a fish feels is uncertain. Touch is probably the least sensitive of a fish's senses.

3

Metabolism: How Fishes Function

 In living things, food fuels metabolism, the chemical processes in cells that are essential to life. An animal's body breaks down food during digestion. The products of digestion are rebuilt into protoplasm, the material that makes up living cells. Protoplasm enables the body to grow and repair itself.

In cells, sugars and other substances obtained from the breakdown of food also combine with oxygen taken in by the body. This reaction generates the energy a body needs to function.

Feeding and breathing, therefore, are the keys to life. This is true not just for fish, but for all animals.

What Fishes Eat

Almost all fishes eat other animals. The prey of various fish species includes other fishes, mammals, and even birds. Fishes also eat invertebrates (animals

Opposite:
A smooth trunkfish blows into the sand to uncover food. Most fishes have diets that include some kind of other animal. Their diets may include mammals, birds, insects, clams, and other fishes, as well as plants.

without backbones, such as insects, crustaceans, clams, and worms). In fact, just about everything living in the water can be a meal for some kind of fish.

Plankton-Feeders

Some fishes also eat plants. The most important plants for the fish food chain are the smallest plants on Earth. They are the microscopic and the near-microscopic plants that float in the water. Together with animals of similar size, they are called plankton.

Ironically, some of the largest fishes feed mostly on the world's smallest plants. The whale shark and the basking shark, which can grow to lengths of 50 feet (15 meters) and weigh as much as 25 tons (22,700 kilograms), dine mainly on plankton.

Among other fishes that feed on plankton are herrings and shad. To eat, they open their mouths and swim through their food. Water filled with plankton passes into their mouths and over their gills. Then the water flows out, but the plankton stays behind.

The basking shark is one of the largest fishes that eat plankton almost exclusively. The basking shark's extremely long gills sift plankton from the water as it passes through the mouth.

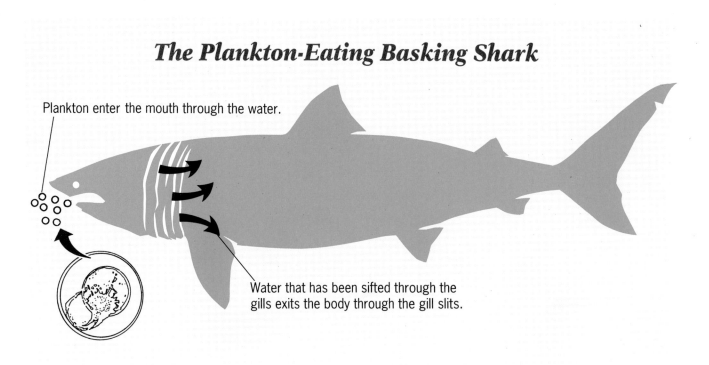

The Plankton-Eating Basking Shark

Plankton enter the mouth through the water.

Water that has been sifted through the gills exits the body through the gill slits.

Stiff, bony structures in the gills sift the plankton from the water so the fishes can swallow it. These structures, which usually resemble combs, are called gill rakers. They also protect the gills from clogging with plankton and dirt.

Fruit-Eaters and Grazers

In the Amazon River basin of South America are fishes that live largely on fruit. One is the pacu, sometimes kept in home aquariums.

Seasonally, the Amazon River floods the Amazon forest. The fishes move into the flooded forest and eat fruit that falls from the trees. For half the year, they stuff themselves on fruit. Indians of the Amazon use fruit as bait to catch fishes.

Cichlids are another kind of fish kept in home aquariums. Certain cichlids in large African lakes graze on algae growing on rocks. The chisel-edged teeth of these fish are adapted to scrape algae off hard surfaces.

The teeth of the parrot fish are fused into one sharp, beak-like structure that is adapted for biting and crushing coral. The parrot fish eats plants and animals that live in and on the coral.

The teeth of saltwater parrot fishes are fused into a sharp "beak." The beak is adapted for biting and crushing coral, but parrot fishes do not eat the coral itself. They eat the living things that grow on and in the coral. Some parrot fishes eat seaweed. Others feed on the small, soft animals that make the coral, called polyps.

The Teeth and Diet of Fishes

Plant-eating fishes usually have molar teeth adapted for grinding up vegetable matter. Those that feed on vertebrates and large invertebrates, especially other fishes, have sharp teeth that are knife-like or curved.

There are similar teeth adaptations in mammals. A horse has flat molars for grinding grasses, but a lion has long canines that knife into prey and blade-like incisors that cut up meat before it is swallowed.

The teeth of the great white shark, which tears chunks out of large prey, are broad and edged like a saw blade. The sand shark eats smaller fishes, crabs, and lobsters. Its teeth are like curved spikes and are ideal for holding wiggly prey.

The Super Predator

Most sharks hunt other vertebrates, especially fishes. Some species of sharks also eat sea lions, sea turtles, sea birds, and dolphins.

Sharks are among the most primitive of fishes. Nonetheless, they may be the most efficient hunters in all the sea. Sharks have been described as "eating machines" and "super predators." They provide a dramatic example of how a fish uses a combination of senses to hunt food.

The sense that is first used depends somewhat on the distance between the shark and its prey. Sharks seem able to pick up a scent that is more than 1 mile

(2 kilometers) away. Their hearing can reach beyond 1,000 feet (305 meters). Their lateral line is sensitive to objects that are about 100 feet (31 meters) away, and their vision is so keen that they can see objects that are about 50 feet (15 meters) away.

Sharks are one of nature's most efficient predators. Some sharks can smell a scent that is more than 1 mile (2 kilometers) away.

If a shark catches a whiff of a possible meal, it may follow the scent up current toward its source. Or an odor may be only a signal that starts the shark searching. Either way, as the shark moves closer, its ears tune in to the target. As it gets even closer, the lateral line begins sensing vibrations. Once a shark sees its prey, it goes in for the kill. This has worked perfectly for millions of years.

Digestion

After a fish eats, it digests much like a human or other vertebrate. Digestion begins in the stomach, which is often U-shaped. The stomach's muscular walls

There is a fish that shoots down its prey, like a hunter gunning down a bird. The archerfish spits a jet of water at insects sitting on bushes that overhang the water. The archerfish is a deadly marksman. When the water jet knocks an insect into the water, the archerfish pounces.

Another fish actually "fishes for fish." The anglerfish has a fleshy tab on its head that is a living fishing lure. To attract its prey, the anglerfish lies on the ocean floor and wiggles its tab. Other fishes mistake it for a worm or another small creature. They come looking for a meal but, instead, they become one, when the anglerfish opens its huge mouth and gulps them down.

An anglerfish has a fleshy tab on its head that attracts fishes.

An archerfish shoots water at an insect nearby.

grind up food that has been swallowed. Meanwhile, glands secrete acids that chemically reduce food to nutrients that are usable by the body.

How Fishes Breathe

Organs called gills are other features of fishes. Gills enable fishes to breathe oxygen dissolved in water. Oxygen from the air enters water at the surface. Aquatic algae also produce oxygen.

Gills are usually just behind a fish's eye, on each side of the body. They are made of delicate, folded tissues that contain tiny blood vessels. These vessels carry deoxygenated blood from the heart.

Blood in a fish's gills is separated from the water by a wall only one cell thick. Oxygen passes from the water into the blood. Then it goes to the heart, which is shaped like a tube. The heart pumps oxygen-rich blood to the rest of the body. After body cells use up the blood's oxygen during metabolism, the blood returns to the heart. It then pumps the blood back to the gills, where more oxygen enters the blood.

In living things, carbon dioxide gas is produced as a waste during bodily processes. In fishes, carbon dioxide is carried to the gills by deoxygenated blood. As the oxygen from water recharges the blood, carbon dioxide is released from the blood into the water as waste. This entire process is called respiration.

Body Temperature

Fishes are generally said to be "cold-blooded animals." This term can be misleading. It suggests that a fish, unlike a bird or mammal, cannot produce body heat. That isn't exactly true.

Actually, a fish's body does generate a little heat. But fishes do not produce nearly as much heat as birds or mammals. Nor are fishes covered by fur or feathers that protect against heat loss. This means a fish's body temperature varies with its surroundings, just as it does in all cold-blooded animals.

There are a few exceptions to the cold-blooded rule. Tunas, for example, are packed with powerful muscles that make them one of the fastest fishes. The action of all this muscle contracting and relaxing produces considerable heat, making tunas almost warm-blooded.

How Fishes Breathe

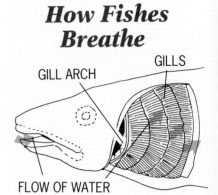

Most fishes have four gills on each side of the head. Water enters the mouth and flows out through the gills. Each gill is made up of fleshy, thread-like filaments.

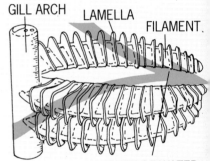

Water from the mouth passes over the filaments, which are closely spaced along a gill arch in two rows. Three of the many filaments of a gill are shown above.

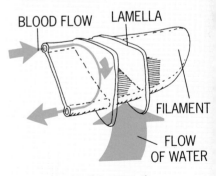

Each filament has many tiny extensions called lamellae. Blood flowing through a lamella takes oxygen from the water and releases carbon dioxide into the water.

Metabolism: How Fishes Function

4

Reproduction and Growth

Eating, breathing, digesting, sensing, and moving are the functions that help all animals survive. Another key function of animal survival is called reproduction, or breeding. Reproduction helps living things survive by making more members of the species. A species will continue to exist as long as the number of new adults gained from reproduction equals those lost to death.

Reproduction in Fishes

Fishes reproduce their species in the same basic manner as humans and the other vertebrates. For reproduction, a male sex cell, the sperm, unites with a female sex cell, the egg. This is called fertilization. When fertilization takes place, a new organism is created.

In mammals, birds, and some reptiles, fertilization occurs within the female's body. The male sex

The male seahorse has a pouch on his abdomen that is used to hatch its young. Here, a male seahorse is "giving birth" to hatched baby seahorses.

organ, the penis, is inserted into the female's vagina. A sperm from the penis unites with the egg inside the female. Eventually, the fertilized egg winds up in a chamber called the uterus.

The eggs of the vast majority of fishes are not fertilized inside the female. Most fish eggs are fertilized in the water. Males and females simply release sperm (milt) and eggs. Those eggs that come into contact with sperm are fertilized.

Breeding

Some fishes pair off with just one fish. Others pair off with a few fishes for breeding. Most fishes, however, breed in groups. Sometimes these groups are made up of hundreds of fishes. Breeding takes energy. Some fishes put their energy into laying vast numbers of eggs. Others produce fewer eggs, but use their energy to take care of them.

Each fish species has a particular time when it is ready to breed. This is when the greatest number of individual fishes are producing eggs or sperm.

Cod, for instance, breed in winter and early spring. Scientists suspect that the winter's cold water temperatures stimulate the cod to reproduce.

Mass Reproduction

Together, a large group of cod, called a cod mass, produces eggs. A single female can lay up to 9 million eggs in a season. During breeding season, cod gather in huge schools. Males and females swim close together, releasing sperm and eggs at the same time.

Billions of eggs cloud the water. The cod ignore them, except perhaps to eat them. Only one egg in a million will end up as an adult cod. However, since each female cod produces such a huge number of eggs, the one-in-a-million rate is enough to create the next generation of cod adults.

Caring for the Young

Angelfishes pair off to reproduce. They carefully guard their eggs and, later, their young. This type of behavior is more common among freshwater fishes than among those of the ocean.

Male and female angelfishes are caring parents. The female lays few eggs—usually only a couple of dozen—but both parents work hard to help their young survive.

The female angelfish places her eggs on the leaves of various water plants. There, the male fertilizes them. Then both parents use their fins to fan water over the eggs. This keeps them clean and gives them oxygen.

Angelfishes pair off to reproduce and spend much time guarding their eggs. They also take much care to protect their young and help ensure their survival.

Each hatchling angel-fish hangs from its leaf by a sticky thread on its head. Every hour or so, for two days, the parents suck up mouthfuls of young, then spray them on their leaves. This way, dirt and germs do not accumulate on the young. If a hatchling falls from a leaf, a parent picks it up and puts it back. When

5

Fitting into the Web of Life

As fishes develop from eggs to adults, they play various parts in the water world's web of life. Throughout its days, a fish interacts with other animals and its environment.

Food Chains and Food Webs

A food chain is made up of a series of organisms that feed on one another in an ecosystem. A network of overlapping food chains is called a food web. The food web of the aquatic world is a complex one.

All food webs begin with the flow of energy, in the form of sunlight. Plants use sunlight to make food and, ultimately, living tissue. Animals eat plants. That is the way it is on land and in the water.

In the sea, plants in plankton are the "primary producers" of food. They are the first elements in any food chain. These plants are eaten by tiny animals and, as we have learned, by large plankton-eaters like the whale shark, too.

As larvae, many fishes eat plankton. The larvae are then eaten by bigger fishes. As young fishes grow,

Opposite:
A pink anemone fish weaves in and out of the brightly colored tentacles of an anemone. Living things survive by adapting in many ways to their unique environments.

An Ocean Food Chain

A. Sunlight filters through water, stimulating the growth of microscopic plant life, such as algae.

B. Small animal life feeds on the algae. Together, the small plants and animals are called plankton.

C. Small fish feed on plankton.

D, E. The smaller fish (D) are eaten by the larger fish (E).

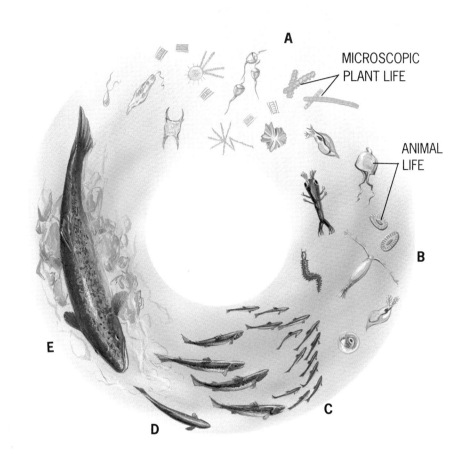

MICROSCOPIC PLANT LIFE

ANIMAL LIFE

they prey on the various animals that are smaller than they are. And then larger animals prey on them.

At the top of many food chains are big predators—fish such as the great white shark and mammals such as the killer whale.

Competition for Food

Fishes compete with other fishes and other animals for food. These other animals often include birds and humans that take fish from the sea for food.

The bluefish is a medium-size, aggressive predator that hunts in large schools. Some people call bluefish "choppers" because they literally chop smaller fish to pieces with razor-sharp teeth.

When bluefishes swarm into an area, they can sweep it clean of smaller fishes. Then there is less to eat for other fish consumers, such as cod and seals.

Bluefishes often attack and eat Atlantic mackerel. During the 1870s, bluefishes were especially abundant off the coast of New England, where they are still common. Bluefishes killed so many mackerel that commercial fishers, who depended on mackerel catches, hated the bluefish.

Bluefishes themselves are hunted by sharks. Sand sharks sometimes gather around bluefishes and herd them into tight schools. Then the sharks tear into them, which is exactly what bluefishes commonly do to smaller fishes.

Prey and Predator

In addition to reproduction, eating and not being eaten are the keys to survival for most animals. The predators that hunt fishes span the animal kingdom. Fishing spiders and dragonfly larvae eat minnows.

An ocean lamprey feeds on a recent catch. In the ocean habitat, fishes compete with other fishes and other animals for food.

With their powerful eyes, bald eagles are extremely good fishers. Many animals, such as birds, bears, and humans, rely upon fishes for food.

A stonefish lies motionless, waiting for prey to approach. Many fishes have evolved adaptations that allow them to blend into their various surroundings. These adaptations enable a fish both to hide from its predators and to surprise its prey.

Jellyfishes, garter snakes, herons, eagles, otters, and sea lions also feed on different fishes. Even bears and humans make fish a large part of their diets.

Fishes prey on some things that may surprise you. The marine goosefish sometimes eats aquatic birds. So does the wels, a European catfish that can be as long as 10 feet (3 meters). A hare was once found in a cod's stomach; largemouth bass grab swimming mice.

Color, Shape, and Behavior

Fishes have a wide variety of adaptations that help them prey on other animals. Many of these same adaptations also keep them safe.

Color, shape, and behavior help a fish eat and avoid being eaten. The frogfish, for example, is the same color as certain seaweeds. Its body is covered with tabs and other appendages that resemble the branches of seaweed. Surrounded by seaweed, unmoving, the frogfish is difficult to detect. It hides from predators and lies in ambush for prey.

The stonefish, of the Indian and Pacific oceans, looks like a hunk of old coral. It can lie "invisible" on a coral reef, waiting to snap up smaller fishes that do not detect it.

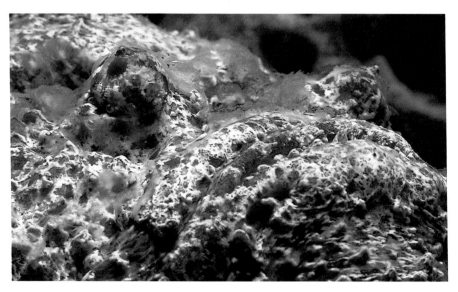

The color, shape, and behavior of the stonefish also protect it by hiding it from enemies. But it has another type of protection, too. On its back are spines with a powerful poison, or venom. Some people who have stepped on a stonefish have died within minutes.

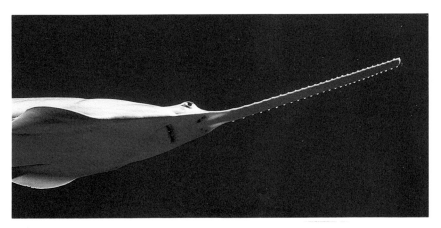

Over millions of years, the sawfish has adapted to life in the ocean by evolving a long, sawlike snout that can slash at prey and defend against enemies.

The lionfish is another fish that has poisonous spines. If threatened, it spreads its fins and displays vivid maroon and cream stripes. Predators that have tangled with lionfishes before recognize those color patterns and heed the warning.

Changing Color

Cells containing color pigments are distributed over the skin of a fish. The colors in these cells may be orange, red, yellow, or black. These pigments can be spread out or squeezed into a dot. By moving their pigments, fishes can increase or decrease the size of their stripes or spots. And the basic colors can be combined to form others.

Changing color is another way many fishes better survive in the ocean environment. Some fishes can actually change color at will in order to better blend into their various surroundings. The winter flounder, shown here, either covers itself with sand or changes its top coloring when it lies flat on the sea floor.

A moray is cleaned by a small group of cleaner gobies. Sometimes, different species form partnerships that allow each certain advantages. Cleaner gobies, for instance, help to keep the moray free of parasites while, at the same time, they get a source of food and protection.

Certain fishes increase their natural camouflage by changing colors to match surroundings. The flounder is very good at this natural disguise. When on black mud, the flounder turns itself black. On yellow sand, the fish changes to yellow. When scientists placed a flounder on a black-and-white checkerboard during a laboratory experiment, the fish was able to match the checkerboard pattern perfectly!

Associations with Other Creatures

Associations with other animals help some fishes survive. The sea anemone is a relative of the jellyfish. Like its relative, the anemone stings small fishes with its tentacles and eats them. But the brightly colored little clownfish lives unharmed among the anemone's tentacles, which offer shelter from bigger fishes. You would think the clownfish would get stung, but it doesn't. Something—perhaps a coating of mucus—protects the clownfish against the stingers.

Sometimes the association between fishes is a partnership, benefiting both animals. Several species of small marine fishes, called "cleaner" fishes, eat parasites off larger fishes. With this partnership, cleaner fishes get food, and the big fishes are freed from parasites.

The big fishes even let cleaners into their mouths so the cleaners can look for parasites there. Normally, the big fishes would eat the smaller fishes. But the big fishes do not eat cleaners. Scientists believe big fishes can recognize color patterns on the cleaners and can sense not to eat them.

Big fishes also congregate in places where cleaner fishes live. Concentrations of big fishes at the "cleaning station" can influence the distribution of big fishes in the sea. In this way, the cleaners have a major impact on the entire ocean environment.

The Conservation of Fishes

Like all other life on the planet, fishes are suffering from the impact of human activity on the environment. According to scientists, on North America alone, more than 300 species of freshwater fishes are in danger of extinction. That's a third of the total number inhabiting the continent.

These fishes include a wide variety of species—little ones hardly anybody has heard of and those like Pacific salmon, the basis of a fishing industry worth hundreds of millions of dollars. Off the Atlantic coast, flounder, haddock, and other important food fishes are also dwindling fast.

There are many causes for the shrinking fish population. Pollution, dams on rivers, and land development are some of the chief causes. Another big problem is that fishes have been harvested from the oceans faster than they can reproduce to make up for the loss.

Fishes have survived longer than any other vertebrates. But if their dazzling variety is to continue, they will need help from humans.

Fishes need people, but people also need fishes. Throughout history, fish has been a staple food for humans. The very first human probably caught fishes by hand. Eventually, people developed tools for catching fishes. Scientists have discovered fishhooks in Europe that are 20,000 years old. The hooks are made of bone. Primitive peoples also made hooks of stone and wood.

Protecting Fishes

Today, fishes are still a very important source of food, maybe more than ever. Fishes are a good source of protein, an element desperately needed by hungry people in developing countries. Although fishes are

Although fishes are an important source of food for people, overfishing by commercial interests has greatly reduced the world's fish population. To prevent eventual extinction of many species, people must take an active role in protecting and preserving the delicate natural balance of the world's oceans.

Pest Control: The Mosquito Fish

In the southeastern United States lives a little fish that has been used around the world for pest control. It is the mosquito fish. It gets its name because its favorite food is mosquito larvae, which live on the water's surface. Mosquito fishes are a natural form of pest control.

an important source of food for humans, many problems have been created by humans who take too much fish from the sea. Overfishing by humans has greatly reduced the world's population of fishes. The number of bluefin tuna off the east coast of North America, for example, dropped from a million in 1970 to about 200,000 in 1992. That is a striking decrease of 80 percent in only 20 years.

Fishery experts and environmental activists are working on plans to reverse the decline of food fishes. Today, restrictions are placed on how many of a key species can be caught. But protecting fish species takes more than laws and good intentions. It also takes international cooperation and world education about the importance of wildlife conservation. We all must remember that fishes belong to the whole living world, not just to humans.

Classification Chart of Fishes

Kingdom: **Animal**

Phylum: **Chordata**

Classes (three): **Agnatha, Chondrichthyes, Osteichthyes**

Scientists have identified more than 25,000 different species of fishes, which are grouped into three classes. Within those classes are many superorders that further group fishes by common traits. The following are nine superorders that classify some of the most commonly known fish species.

Major Order	*Common Members*	*Distinctive Features*
Pleurotremata	sharks, dogfishes	Cartilaginous fishes; two dorsal fins and one anal fin; large size
Hypotremata	skates, rays, sawfishes	
Clupeichthyes	herrings, sardines, anchovies	Bony fishes; swim bladder connected to wind pipe
Protacanthopterygii	salmon, trout, pike	Soft-finned bony fishes; many deep-sea fishes
Ostariophysi	minnows, tetras, catfishes, carp	Bony fishes, highly varied; 5,000 species; dominant freshwater fishes of the world
Petromyzoniformes	lampreys	Jawless fishes; snake-like body
Myxiniformes	hagfishes	
Paracanthopterygii	cod, hakes, anglerfishes	Less highly evolved bony fishes; spiny-finned; marine-bottom fishes
Acanthopterygii	flying fishes, seahorses, perches, tunas, mackerel, swordfishes, dolphins, barracudas, flatfishes, boxfishes	Highly evolved bony fishes; highly varied; more than 8,000 species

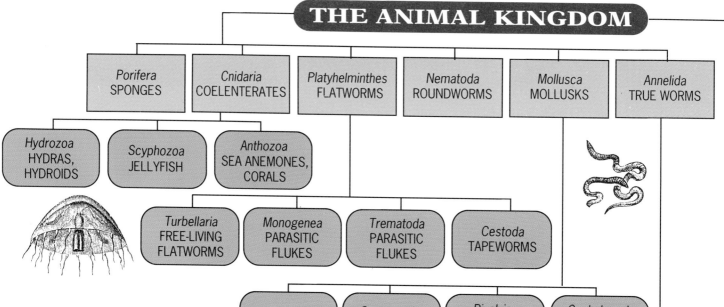

THE ANIMAL KINGDOM

| Porifera SPONGES | Cnidaria COELENTERATES | Platyhelminthes FLATWORMS | Nematoda ROUNDWORMS | Mollusca MOLLUSKS | Annelida TRUE WORMS |

Cnidaria
- Hydrozoa HYDRAS, HYDROIDS
- Scyphozoa JELLYFISH
- Anthozoa SEA ANEMONES, CORALS

Platyhelminthes
- Turbellaria FREE-LIVING FLATWORMS
- Monogenea PARASITIC FLUKES
- Trematoda PARASITIC FLUKES
- Cestoda TAPEWORMS

Mollusca
- Polyplacophora CHITONS
- Gastropoda SNAILS, SLUGS
- Bivalvia CLAMS, SCALLOPS MUSSELS
- Cephalopoda OCTOPUSES, SQUID

Annelida
- Polychaeta MARINE WORMS
- Oligochaeta EARTHWORMS, FRESHWATER WORMS
- Hirudinea LEECHES

Biological Classification

The branch of biology that deals with classification is called taxonomy, or systematics. Biological classification is the arrangement of living organisms into categories. Biologists have created a universal system of classification that they can share with one another, no matter where they study or what language they speak. The categories in a classification chart are based on the natural similarities of the organisms. The similarities considered are the structure of the organism, the development (reproduction and growth), biochemical and physiological functions (metabolism and senses), and evolutionary history. Biologists classify living things to show relationships between different groups of organisms, both ancient and modern. Classification charts are also useful in tracing the evolutionary pathways along which present-day organisms have evolved.

Over the years, the classification process has been altered as new information has become accepted. A long time ago, biologists used a two-kingdom system of classification; every living thing was considered a member of either the plant kingdom or the animal kingdom. Today, many biologists use a five-kingdom system that includes plants, animals, monera (microbes), protista (protozoa and certain molds), and fungi (non-green plants). In every kingdom, however, the hierarchy of classification remains the same. In this chart, groupings go from the most general categories (at the top) down to groups that are more and more specific. The most general grouping is PHYLUM. The most specific is ORDER. To use the chart, you may want to find the familiar name of an organism in a CLASS or ORDER box and then trace its classification upward until you reach its PHYLUM.

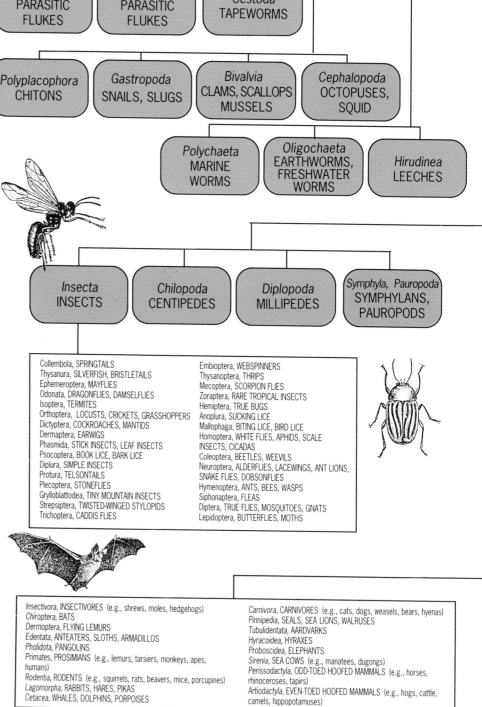

| Insecta INSECTS | Chilopoda CENTIPEDES | Diplopoda MILLIPEDES | Symphyla, Pauropoda SYMPHYLANS, PAUROPODS |

Insecta

Collembola, SPRINGTAILS
Thysanura, SILVERFISH, BRISTLETAILS
Ephemeroptera, MAYFLIES
Odonata, DRAGONFLIES, DAMSELFLIES
Isoptera, TERMITES
Orthoptera, LOCUSTS, CRICKETS, GRASSHOPPERS
Dictyptera, COCKROACHES, MANTIDS
Dermaptera, EARWIGS
Phasmida, STICK INSECTS, LEAF INSECTS
Psocoptera, BOOK LICE, BARK LICE
Diplura, SIMPLE INSECTS
Protura, TELSONTAILS
Plecoptera, STONEFLIES
Grylloblattodea, TINY MOUNTAIN INSECTS
Strepsiptera, TWISTED-WINGED STYLOPIDS
Trichoptera, CADDIS FLIES

Embioptera, WEBSPINNERS
Thysanoptera, THRIPS
Mecoptera, SCORPION FLIES
Zoraptera, RARE TROPICAL INSECTS
Hemiptera, TRUE BUGS
Anoplura, SUCKING LICE
Mallophaga, BITING LICE, BIRD LICE
Homoptera, WHITE FLIES, APHIDS, SCALE INSECTS, CICADAS
Coleoptera, BEETLES, WEEVILS
Neuroptera, ALDERFLIES, LACEWINGS, ANT LIONS, SNAKE FLIES, DOBSONFLIES
Hymenoptera, ANTS, BEES, WASPS
Siphonaptera, FLEAS
Diptera, TRUE FLIES, MOSQUITOES, GNATS
Lepidoptera, BUTTERFLIES, MOTHS

Insectivora, INSECTIVORES (e.g., shrews, moles, hedgehogs)
Chiroptera, BATS
Dermoptera, FLYING LEMURS
Edentata, ANTEATERS, SLOTHS, ARMADILLOS
Pholidota, PANGOLINS
Primates, PROSIMIANS (e.g., lemurs, tarsiers, monkeys, apes, humans)
Rodentia, RODENTS (e.g., squirrels, rats, beavers, mice, porcupines)
Lagomorpha, RABBITS, HARES, PIKAS
Cetacea, WHALES, DOLPHINS, PORPOISES

Carnivora, CARNIVORES (e.g., cats, dogs, weasels, bears, hyenas)
Pinnipedia, SEALS, SEA LIONS, WALRUSES
Tubulidentata, AARDVARKS
Hyracoidea, HYRAXES
Proboscidea, ELEPHANTS
Sirenia, SEA COWS (e.g., manatees, dugongs)
Perissodactyla, ODD-TOED HOOFED MAMMALS (e.g., horses, rhinoceroses, tapirs)
Artiodactyla, EVEN-TOED HOOFED MAMMALS (e.g., hogs, cattle, camels, hippopotamuses)

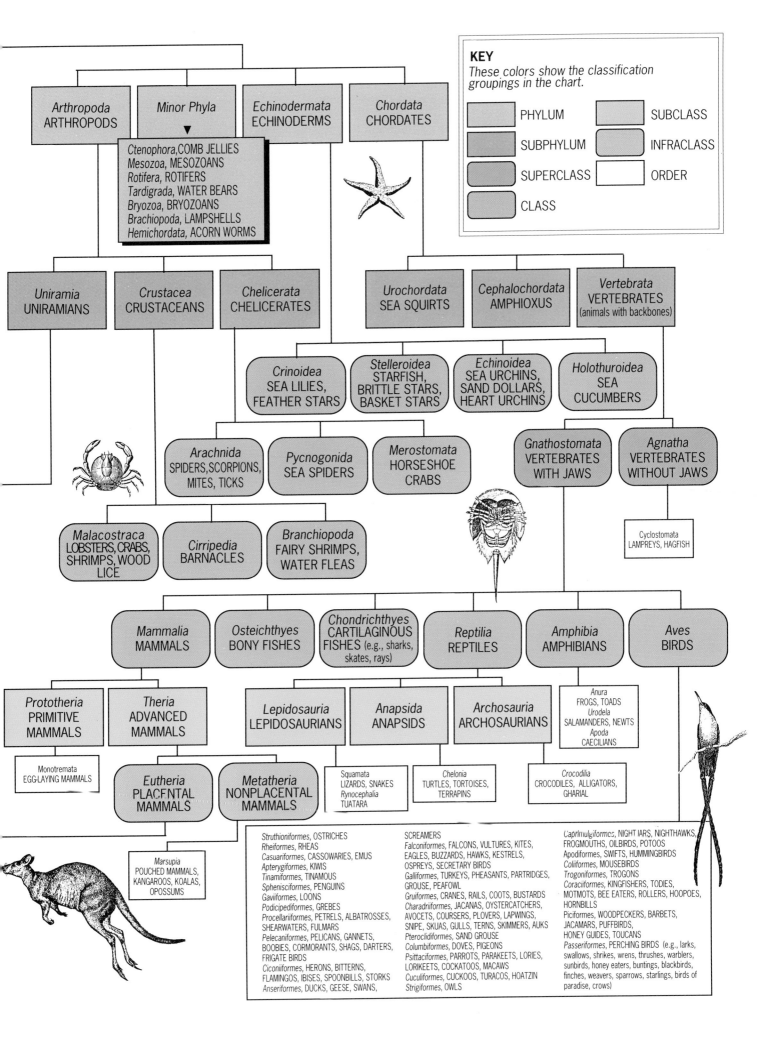

KEY

These colors show the classification groupings in the chart.

- PHYLUM
- SUBPHYLUM
- SUPERCLASS
- CLASS
- SUBCLASS
- INFRACLASS
- ORDER

Arthropoda ARTHROPODS

Minor Phyla
- Ctenophora, COMB JELLIES
- Mesozoa, MESOZOANS
- Rotifera, ROTIFERS
- Tardigrada, WATER BEARS
- Bryozoa, BRYOZOANS
- Brachiopoda, LAMPSHELLS
- Hemichordata, ACORN WORMS

Echinodermata ECHINODERMS

Chordata CHORDATES

Uniramia UNIRAMIANS

Crustacea CRUSTACEANS

Chelicerata CHELICERATES

Urochordata SEA SQUIRTS

Cephalochordata AMPHIOXUS

Vertebrata VERTEBRATES (animals with backbones)

Crinoidea SEA LILIES, FEATHER STARS

Stelleroidea STARFISH, BRITTLE STARS, BASKET STARS

Echinoidea SEA URCHINS, SAND DOLLARS, HEART URCHINS

Holothuroidea SEA CUCUMBERS

Arachnida SPIDERS, SCORPIONS, MITES, TICKS

Pycnogonida SEA SPIDERS

Merostomata HORSESHOE CRABS

Gnathostomata VERTEBRATES WITH JAWS

Agnatha VERTEBRATES WITHOUT JAWS

Malacostraca LOBSTERS, CRABS, SHRIMPS, WOOD LICE

Cirripedia BARNACLES

Branchiopoda FAIRY SHRIMPS, WATER FLEAS

Cyclostomata LAMPREYS, HAGFISH

Mammalia MAMMALS

Osteichthyes BONY FISHES

Chondrichthyes CARTILAGINOUS FISHES (e.g., sharks, skates, rays)

Reptilia REPTILES

Amphibia AMPHIBIANS

Aves BIRDS

Prototheria PRIMITIVE MAMMALS

Theria ADVANCED MAMMALS

Lepidosauria LEPIDOSAURIANS

Anapsida ANAPSIDS

Archosauria ARCHOSAURIANS

Anura FROGS, TOADS
Urodela SALAMANDERS, NEWTS
Apoda CAECILIANS

Monotremata EGG-LAYING MAMMALS

Eutheria PLACENTAL MAMMALS

Metatheria NONPLACENTAL MAMMALS

Squamata LIZARDS, SNAKES
Rynocephalia TUATARA

Chelonia TURTLES, TORTOISES, TERRAPINS

Crocodilia CROCODILES, ALLIGATORS, GHARIAL

Marsupia POUCHED MAMMALS, KANGAROOS, KOALAS, OPOSSUMS

Struthioniformes, OSTRICHES
Rheiformes, RHEAS
Casuariiformes, CASSOWARIES, EMUS
Apterygiformes, KIWIS
Tinamiformes, TINAMOUS
Sphenisciformes, PENGUINS
Gaviiformes, LOONS
Podicipediformes, GREBES
Procellariiformes, PETRELS, ALBATROSSES, SHEARWATERS, FULMARS
Pelecaniformes, PELICANS, GANNETS, BOOBIES, CORMORANTS, SHAGS, DARTERS, FRIGATE BIRDS
Ciconiiformes, HERONS, BITTERNS, FLAMINGOS, IBISES, SPOONBILLS, STORKS
Anseriformes, DUCKS, GEESE, SWANS,

SCREAMERS
Falconiformes, FALCONS, VULTURES, KITES, EAGLES, BUZZARDS, HAWKS, KESTRELS, OSPREYS, SECRETARY BIRDS
Galliformes, TURKEYS, PHEASANTS, PARTRIDGES, GROUSE, PEAFOWL
Gruiformes, CRANES, RAILS, COOTS, BUSTARDS
Charadriiformes, JACANAS, OYSTERCATCHERS, AVOCETS, COURSERS, PLOVERS, LAPWINGS, SNIPE, SKUAS, GULLS, TERNS, SKIMMERS, AUKS
Pteroclidiformes, SAND GROUSE
Columbiformes, DOVES, PIGEONS
Psittaciformes, PARROTS, PARAKEETS, LORIES, LORIKEETS, COCKATOOS, MACAWS
Cuculiformes, CUCKOOS, TURACOS, HOATZIN
Strigiformes, OWLS

Caprimulgiformes, NIGHTJARS, NIGHTHAWKS, FROGMOUTHS, OILBIRDS, POTOOS
Apodiformes, SWIFTS, HUMMINGBIRDS
Coliiformes, MOUSEBIRDS
Trogoniformes, TROGONS
Coraciiformes, KINGFISHERS, TODIES, MOTMOTS, BEE EATERS, ROLLERS, HOOPOES, HORNBILLS
Piciformes, WOODPECKERS, BARBETS, JACAMARS, PUFFBIRDS, HONEY GUIDES, TOUCANS
Passeriformes, PERCHING BIRDS (e.g., larks, swallows, shrikes, wrens, thrushes, warblers, sunbirds, honey eaters, buntings, blackbirds, finches, weavers, sparrows, starlings, birds of paradise, crows)

Glossary

adaptation The body part or behavior that helps an organism survive in its environment.

appendage A body part attached to another body part.

aquatic Adapted to life in water.

barbels Feelers on the outside of some fishes' snouts, used for tasting and touching.

camouflage The colors, shapes, or structures that enable an organism to blend with its surroundings.

cartilage Skeletal material of some fishes, softer and more flexible than bone.

cloaca The opening in some female fishes into which a male inserts a penis-like tube for fertilization.

cones Light-sensitive cells in the eye that are most sensitive in bright light and register color.

digestion The mechanical and chemical breakdown of food into substances the body can use for growth and energy.

ecosystem A system formed by the interaction of a community of organisms with their environment.

embryo The young animal developing within an egg.

extinct No longer in existence.

fertilization The union of sperm and egg, which leads to the development of a new organism.

food chain The order in which a series of organisms feed on one another in an ecosystem.

food web A system of overlapping and interconnected food chains.

gills The organs that a fish uses to breathe in water.

invertebrate An animal without a backbone.

iris A covering for the lens of the eye that channels light to the lens.

larva A newly hatched fish.

lateral line An organ along each side of a fish's body that senses very low vibrations.

lens A clear structure at the center of the eye through which light passes to the retina.

metabolism The chemical processes in cells that are essential to life.

milt Fish sperm.

motor nerves Nerves that carry messages from the brain and spinal cord to the muscles.

olfactory Having to do with the sense of smell.

optic nerve One of a pair of nerves that send visual stimuli to the brain.

parr A young salmon, approximately 4 inches (10 centimeters) long.

pigment A coloring matter in plant and animal cells or tissues.

plankton Microscopic and near-microscopic plants and animals in water.

polyps Small animals that make coral.

predator An animal that kills other animals for food.

prey Animals that are eaten by other animals.

protoplasm The material that makes up living cells.

redd Spawning area.

reproduction The process by which organisms create other members of their species.

respiration The exchange of gases between an organism and its environment; the use of oxygen for the tissues and cells of the body.

retina A light-sensitive coating on the back of the eye, like the film of a camera.

rods Light-sensitive cells in the back of the eye that are most sensitive in dim light and register only black and white.

school A group of fish that stay together, without a leader.

sensory nerves Nerves that carry messages from the sense organs to the brain.

spawning Producing or depositing eggs.

species A group of organisms that share more traits with one another than with other organisms and that can reproduce with one another.

sperm The male reproductive cell that fertilizes a female egg.

stimuli Messages received by an animal's senses from its surroundings.

uterus The female organ in which the embryo develops.

vertebrate An animal with a backbone.

For Further Reading

Arnold, Caroline. *Watch Out for Sharks*. New York: Clarion Books, 1991.

Bailey, Jill, and Seddon, Tony. *Animal Parenting*. New York: Facts On File, 1989.

Baker, Lucy. *Life in the Oceans*. New York: Franklin Watts, 1990.

Brooks, Bruce. *Nature by Design*. New York: Farrar, 1991.

Brooks, Bruce. *Predator*. New York: Farrar, 1991.

Cherfas, Jeremy. *Animal Communications*. Minneapolis: Lerner Publications, 1991.

Cherfas, Jeremy. *Animal Defenses*. Minneapolis: Lerner Publications, 1991.

Cherfas, Jeremy. *Animal Societies*. Minneapolis: Lerner Publications, 1991.

Colin, Patrick. *Marine Invertebrates and Plants of the Living Reef*. Neptune, NJ: TFH Publications, 1988.

Coupe, Sheena. *Sharks*. New York: Facts On File, 1990.

Oram, Liz, and Baker, Robin. *Migration at Sea*. Milwaukee: Raintree Steck-Vaughn, 1992.

Parker, Steve. *Fish* (Eyewitness Books). New York: Alfred A. Knopf, 1990.

Peissel, Michel, and Allen, Missy. *Dangerous Water Creatures*. New York: Chelsea House Publications, 1992.

Tesar, Jenny. *Threatened Oceans*. New York: Facts On File, 1991.

Index

Photo Credits
Cover and title page: ©Y. Lanceau Jacana/Photo Researchers, Inc; p.6: ©Andrew Martinez/Photo Researchers, Inc; p.8: ©Mike Neumann/Photo Researchers, Inc; p.9 (left): ©Spencer Grant/Photo Researchers, Inc; p.9 (right): ©Hans Reinhard/OKAPIA/Photo Researchers, Inc; p.13: Steinhart Aquarium (©Tom McHugh/Photo Researchers, Inc); p.16: ©Tom McHugh/Photo Researchers, Inc; p. 17: Dallas Aquarium/Photo Researchers, Inc; p. 18: ©Fred McConnaughey/Photo Researchers, Inc; p.19: ©David Hall/Photo Researchers, Inc; p.21 (top): ©J.W. Mowbray/Photo Researchers, Inc; p.21 (bottom): ©Mike Neumann/Photo Researchers, Inc; p.22: ©William H. Mullins/Photo Researchers, Inc; p.28: ©R.J. Erwin/Photo Researchers, Inc; p.30: ©William H. Mullins/Photo Researchers, Inc; p.31: ©Alvin E. Staffan/Photo Researchers, Inc; p.32: Steinhart Aquarium (©Tom McHugh/Photo Researchers, Inc); p. 33: ©Fred McConnaughey/Photo Researchers, Inc; p.34: ©David Hall/Photo Researchers, Inc; p.37: ©Charles V. Angelo/Photo Researchers, Inc; p.39: ©Tom McHugh/Photo Researchers, Inc; p.40: ©Roy Pinney/Photo Researchers, Inc; p.40 (inset): ©Charles V. Angelo/Photo Researchers, Inc; p.42: ©Bill Curtsinger/Photo Researchers, Inc; p. 44: ©Dr. Paul A. Zahl/Photo Researchers, Inc; p.45: ©Jeanne White/Photo Researchers, Inc; p.48: ©Fred McConnaughey/Photo Researchers, Inc; p.51: ©Berthoule-Scott/Photo Researchers, Inc; p. 52 (top): ©Tom and Pat Leeson/ Photo Researchers, Inc; p.52 (bottom): Steinhart Aquarium (©Tom McHugh/Photo Researchers, Inc); p. 53 (top): Steinhart Aquarium (©Tom McHugh/Photo Researchers, Inc); p. 53 (bottom): ©Andrew Martinez/Photo Researchers, Inc; p.54: ©Nancy Sefton/Photo Researchers, Inc; p. 55: ©Ronny Jaques/Photo Researchers, Inc; p.56: ©Robert Noonan/Photo Researchers, Inc.
Technical illustrations: ©Blackbirch Press, Inc.

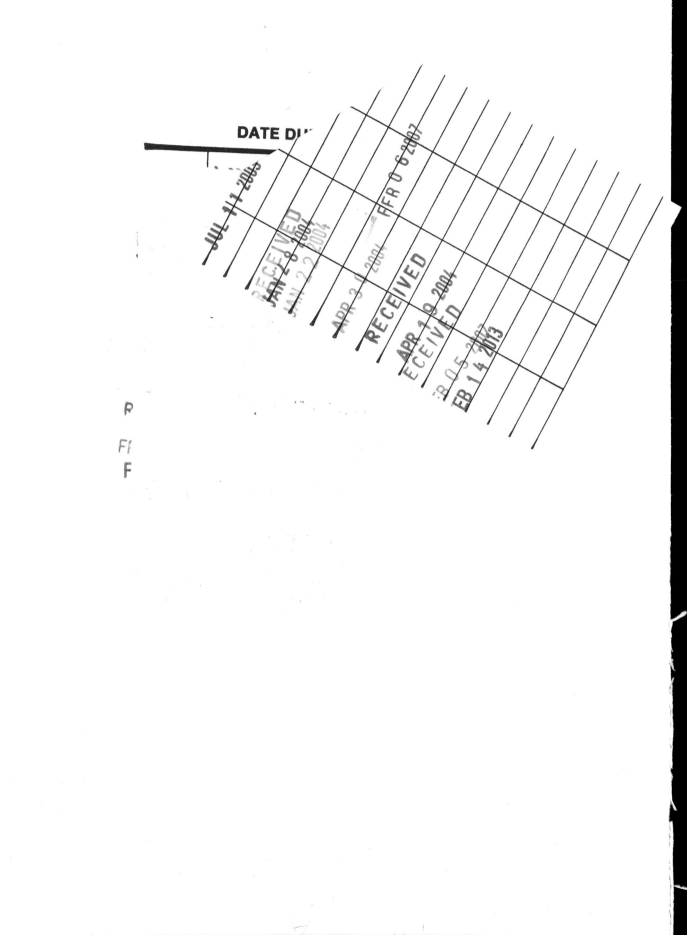